Marine Engine Layup:

A Step-by-Step Guide to Decommissioning, Inboards, Stern drives and Outboard Motors

from the the Editors of
MarineEngineDigest.com

"Good Books Are Where We Find Our Dreams"

Editor@MiddleCoastPublishing.com

© Copyright 1995, 2016 – All rights reserved.

Publisher's Cataloging-in-Publication data
Banse, Timothy P.
  Marine engine lay-up : a step-by-step guide to decommissioning inboards, stern drives, and outboard motors / by Tim Banse. Middle Coast Pub., c2016

978-0-934523-37-0 **PRINT**

978-0-934523-41-7 E-Book

95-30192

Marine Engine Digest's Marine Mechanic Series

DEDICATION

This book is dedicated to my mentor,

Adrian Lundeen,

the grizzled old Swede from the backwater sloughs of the Mississippi River near Albany, Illinois, who instilled in me the value of owning and maintaining quality tools, and who taught me how to work on outboard motors with pride, professionalism and competence.

CONTENTS

How to Use This Book

If you've never laid-up a marine engine before then consider reading this book from cover to cover before you even touch a wrench. This is so you more thoroughly understand the theory behind the methods to be presented.

Once you actually begin to do work, you may find it helpful to work from a checklist. You'll find one for each configuration (outboard, inboard and stern drive) located at the back of the book. Said forms allow you to keep records of which parts you've replaced. Both the checklists and the forms from this book can be found online at:

http://www.MarineEngineDigest.com/lay-up-forms.htm

They can be printed out and photocopied. As you complete each step in laying-up your boat, put a check mark in the appropriate box. That way you will remember exactly where you left off in case you're interrupted, and even more importantly, months from now in the spring, you'll have a record of exactly which chores you completed and those you left for commissioning.

If you're not in the habit of keeping maintenance records, begin to do from now on. Use the checklists and forms we just talked about to log all the important details such as which procedures you've completed, which cylinder's spark plugs were fouled, whether or not the lift pump's oil reservoir required topping off, and so on.

It's also not a bad idea to store receipts for the replacement parts and fogging oil along with the maintenance log. This for the simple reason that it provides further documentation and recollection of your efforts. You should also know that recording keeping accomplishes a number of worthy benefits. First and foremost, it establishes a pattern that simplifies troubleshooting in the inevitable event that something goes haywire.

For example, knowing a lower unit consistently showed water in its lube over the past five winterizations, you won't be surprised when the day comes that the propeller shaft seals finally let go. Or, when one particular cylinder keeps fouling its spark plugs over the past five tune-ups, you'll know to concentrate your troubleshooting efforts on that cylinder without mucking around blindly trying to find the problem.

On the financial side, you'll be able to keep accurate track of exactly how much maintenance is costing. Combine those numbers with fuel and slip space, and you have a rock solid track on total boating costs. Finally, allowing for the fact that someday you might consider selling your boat, motor and trailer, detailed records and receipts can help reassure the buyer that he's investing in a well-maintained rig and not a neglected beater.

Why Winterize?

Winterizing a marine engine is the single-most important maintenance duty a boater can perform. Done correctly in the autumn very little work needs to be done come spring in order to prepare a rig for sea duty. More to the point, winterizing greatly extends the power train's lifespan by protecting all of its varied components from the ravages of corrosion and freezing. Even in a tropical climate laying up an engine is important. While freezing weather isn't a problem, rust is.

Suffice it to say time spent preparing for winter layup will give you peace of mind as the winter gets bitter, and pay big dividends in the spring when you can't wait to get launched for a new season.

Restated for emphasis the goal is to eliminate the possibility of fluids freezing and expanding in heat exchangers and batteries - and thereby exploding; to keep a film of oil coating cylinders, intakes and exhaust to prevent rust; and to maintain fuel in the fuel system to prevent corrosion or damage to seals. No matter what the latitude and longitude, without fogging the cylinders with a protective coating of sticky oil, severe rusting occurs. Even if corrosion doesn't rust the piston rings to the cylinder wall, the pits left behind on start-up hasten wear.

Without the benefit of flushing the cooling system, salt crystals that have precipitated out of the water will have all winter long to corrode internal passages. Don't bother to drain the gear case oil and trapped water can freeze, expand and destroy expensive housings. Tired oil is loaded with acid and it will etch critically machined surfaces shortening engine life. With all that doom and gloom in mind we've prepared a definitive guide for the winterization of stern drive, inboard and outboard motors.

The following procedures are easy to comprehend and even easier to perform. For the most part you probably already own all the tools you'll need to get the job done quickly and efficiently. Your biggest expense will be for spark plugs, essential fluids such as engine oil, gear oil, antifreeze and fogging oil. The cost of those necessities is money well spent, especially when measured against what it would cost to repair the damage if you were too foolishly short change the lay-up procedure.

All things considered, your biggest investment will be your time. Depending on how comfortable you are with tools, and whether yours is a twin or single engine installation, figure on spending anywhere between a morning and a full day to get the job done right. Let's begin.

Stabilize the Fuel

Gasoline's lifespan is finite. Left untreated during the cold winter months, the lighter fuel molecules evaporate leaving behind gum and varnish that clog fuel filters and carburetor passages. When that happens an engine is hard starting, if it will start at all. Serious cases require a complete rebuilding of the carburetor, or even outright replacement.

To avoid that kind of grief all one needs do is treat the fuel with stabilizer. The amount of stabilizer required depends on two variables: The length of time the fuel is to be protected and the number of gallons in the tank. Directions on the can of stabilizer tell how many ounces to add. Usually about a sixteen ounce bottle of concentrated stabilizer will treat about 40 gallons of fuel. If you burn a alcohol blend of E-10 or E-15 fuel use ethanol rated stabilizer, usually called marine grade stabilizer. Wear protective gloves. Use a funnel.

Once the fuel is dosed with the appropriate amount of stabilizer, the gas in the tank is protected, but the gas in the lines, fuel pump and carburetor is not. For this reason, fuel tanks must be dosed before the engine is run for the last time in the fall. That way stabilized gasoline flows into all the systems components, protecting them for the duration. Also, it's best to store the tanks full of fuel to minimize condensation forming in the tanks.

Note: If you are already treating the fuel with octane booster, it may already be stabilized. This for the simple reason some octane boosters pull double duty as stabilizers. If you're not sure whether your octane booster qualifies, consult the manufacturer. But when in doubt, stabilize.

How can you tell if there's water in the gas? Simple. Drop a small amount of the suspected fuel into the palm of your hand. If all of it evaporates, it's gasoline. On the other hand, if little beads of water dot your hand, it's contaminated.

Flame Arrestor Therapy

Stern drive and inboard engines filter air intake through a flame arrestor. Unlike a car's paper filter, a boat's filter element is expanded metal. Besides preventing the ingestion of particulate matter that would cause internal engine wear, the flame arrestor also quenches backfire flame so it doesn't ignite gasoline vapors that may have accumulated in the bilge.

During cylinder fogging procedure on inboard and stern drive engines you will remove the flame arrestor to gain access to the carburetor throat. Clean the arrestor before replacing it. One tried and true method is to soak it in kerosene and then blow it dry with compressed air. Another acceptable method is to spray it with carburetor/choke cleaner. Either technique helps provide an unrestricted airflow and a cleaner running engine. However, the bonus when using the carb cleaner is that it's so much easier to continue on and wash down both the throttle and choke butterfly plates as well as the linkage.

Fog the Cylinders

Fogging oil is available in aerosol cans, or in liquid form by the quart, by the gallon, and for shops, by the five gallon pail. In the case of the latter three, it's intended to be delivered via a trigger pump oil can type squirt gun. Fogging oil is a special formulation that includes volatile corrosion inhibitors (VCI) that protect metals through direct contact and vapor action.

Start the engine. Run it long enough to reach normal operating temperature. At this stage of winter lay-up the gasoline should already be dosed with stabilizer so treated fuel is flowing into the carburetor and fuel pump. With the engine lopping along, shut off the fuel. Just as the engine begins to starve for gasoline, squirt fogging oil down the carburetor throat. Your advance warning that the engine is about to die comes as the revs climb briefly, then begin to fall. At the precise moment the revs begin to climb, immediately squirt fogging oil down the carburetor throat. Squirt a continuous stream until the engine stalls. Then take a break.

Once engine temperature has cooled, remove all of the spark plugs. Then squirt about an ounce of fogging oil through the spark plug hole into each cylinder. With each cylinder dosed with fogging oil, reinstall the spark plugs finger tight. Finger tight, because you'll be removing them again in the spring when it's time to evacuate the fogging oil from the cylinders. Crank the motor through several revolutions in order to thoroughly smear the oil around the cylinder walls and piston rings.

Change Engine Oil While it is Warm

Without an oil change at lay-up, corrosive combustion by-products in suspension in the crankcase will work all winter long on bearings and machined surfaces. For the same reason, cranking the engine for a few minutes after an oil change washes critical surfaces clean of the dirty, clinging oil. Know that marine-grade lubricants (versus merely automotive oil) contain extra corrosion-fighting additives.

Be sure to drain the crankcase oil hot, with all the acids and corrosive elements in suspension, so they spill out along with the dirty oil instead of etching vital ring and bearing surfaces during the winter. At the same time, replace the filter so contaminated oil doesn't foul clean oil.

But before installing the new oil filter, first fill it. That way connecting rod and the crankshaft rod and main bearing journals don't wait for the oil pump to first fill a dry filter before finally sending lubricant through the oil galleys. Another tip: Dab a fingerful of oil around the filter gasket to help it seal against the block. With the new filter in place and the oil-level topped off, restart the engine, check the filter base for leaks.

Here's where you check your handiwork. The test run immediately reveals whether or not you replaced the spark plug cables in their correct order and whether or not the new oil filter's seal is leaking.

Start the engine and run it up to its normal operating

temperature. Assuming you've treated the fuel tanks with stabilizer, this also circulates treated gasoline throughout the fuel system. In the meantime inspect the filter base for a leak, tightening as necessary to stem the flow. Also inspect around the circumference of the valve cover gaskets. If any oil is seeping through the gasket, use a slow hand to snug down each one of the bolts in a cross-pattern. Be careful not to over-tighten the valve cover or it may distort and worsen the leak.

What are the telltale signs that a marine engine is running hot? Lay your hand on the cylinder head. It's normally hot, but shouldn't scorch your hand. You should almost, but not quite, be able to lay your hand on it. Or, in the alternative, splash a handful of water on the cylinder head, If the droplets sizzle like they're dancing on a pancake grill then the engine is definitely too hot.

Now throttle down and kill the engine. Pull the dipstick to make sure the oil level registers full. Once you're certain all systems are A-Okay, you'll run the engine one last time when you shut off the flow of stabilized fuel and fog the cylinders with protective lubricant.

Inboard Transmission Care

For the most part inboard transmissions require very little care and attention. The problem is, they're so trouble-free that all too often they end up forgotten until one component or the other fails. That's why winter lay-up presents the ultimate opportunity to give the transmission the once over. First, check the oil level. On simple gearboxes, usually it's supposed to be even with the bottom threads of the top fill hole. On automatic transmissions, follow manufacturer's recommendation's on changing ATF fluid and filter. If in doubt about your particular make and model, consult the owner's manual.

Even more important, in the event the lubricant needs to be topped-off, make absolutely certain which type gear oil the transmission requires. Again, peruse the pages of the owner's manual for the manufacturer's recommendations. Lay a wrench on the transmission mounting bolts, making sure they are snug. Eyeball the rubber mounts, making sure they haven't cracked, broken or vibrated loose.

Propeller Care

Remove the cotter pin, if there is one, otherwise block the blades with a wooden block to prevent the propeller from turning while you loosen the retaining nut. Slide the propeller off the shaft. Inspect the prop's shock absorber bushing for cracks. If the hub is slipping sometimes the malady shows up as a melted or otherwise mis-shapen rubber hub. Check individual blades for nicks and dings.

If any of the blades are bent or dinged, hammer them back into shape with a rawhide mallet. File smooth any jagged edges, being careful to remove as little metal as possible. Nicks bigger than your thumbnail will have removed a substantial amount of weight form the wheel, affecting its balance. An unbalanced the wheel vibrates which could ultimately cause one of the shafts to crack and break. Besides tearing up the running gear, out of balance propellers also waste fuel and drag down top speed. It's cheaper to buy a replacement propeller than it is to rebuild an entire lower unit.

Coat the propeller shaft with anti-corrosion, marine grade grease, then reinstall the propeller using a new shear pin and cotter pin, if so equipped. Don't be tempted to skimp. Use a new cotter pin. Cotter pins are cheap. Replacing a lost propeller isn't. Use only marine-grade grease.

Gear Case Care

Drain and fill the gear case A gear case should be drained and refilled at least every 100 hours running time, or at the very minimum, every fall during normally scheduled lay-up. Otherwise corrosion can attack the gear set and bearings. Worse than the specter of rusty gears and races, if water remains trapped inside the lower unit and the temperature drops below freezing, the expansion of the ice can crack the housing wide open.

To change the oil in a gear case, unscrew the drain plugs with a long-handled screwdriver. First take out the bottom screw, followed by the top one. Doing it this way keeps the dirty lube from spilling all over your fingers before you are ready. Thanks to the laws of physics, vacuum pressure in the gear case keeps the lube from spilling out until the top screw is removed. Let the used oil run out into the drain pan. A one-gallon plastic milk jug with its top cut off makes for an economical drain pan.

Examine the old lube for signs of water or broken bits of bearing and gear teeth. Signs of water include water droplets, rust or a milky white froth. The presence of water means the propeller shaft seal or shift rod seal is leaking. A few drops are borderline and the condition should be carefully monitored next season. More than an ounce of water means a trip to the repair shop to replace the seal. Regardless, you'll need to check it periodically throughout the season.

To check for metal particles rub some of the oil between your fingers, relying on your senses of sight and touch for detection. An acrid burned smell is a clue that the bearings and gears have been running hot. Can you see or feel any bronze bearing flecks? Look in the bottom of the drain pan for bits of ground up brass and broken-up gear teeth. dipping a magnet in the oil will reveal any gear metal but not aluminum or bronze bushing detritus. Finding any metal fragments in the drain pan requires professional intervention of a marine mechanic.

At the same time you change the lower unit gear oil remove the propeller. While it's off, check the place where the shaft meets its seal. If there's a big wad of mono-filament fish line nested there,you might want to have the stern drive pressure checked. Fish line cuts seals. The whirling gears create high pressure, driving out the oil. When the engine stops, the gear case vacuum sucks in water to fill the void. Water is a notoriously poor lubricant and eroder of gears and bearings.

Before refilling the gear case take the time to count the old drain plug gaskets, making sure none are stuck in their recess. Be advised these little critters display a nasty penchant for stacking one on top of the other, with two typically ending up on one drain plug and none on the other. When that happens, one of the plug seals like it's supposed to and the other one leaks like a sieve.

Refill the gear case from the bottom. Pump in lube until it trickles out through the top vent hole. When it does, screw in the top plug and snug it down tight. This way the vacuum will hold the oil long while you screw in the plug. This method also prevents formation of air pockets inside the gear case which would otherwise create an insufficient volume of lubricant. When oil just begins to trickle out the top hole, slip in the top lug and snug it down. The vacuum will hold the lube long enough for you to remove the spout from the lower fill hole and screw in the plug.

You should also know there are two ways to actually introduce the gear case oil into the housing: Directly from a squeeze tube or bottle, or with a pump. The pump is much neater, with virtually no spill. Cost is minimal. But be sure you adapter threads fit your brand of outboard motor or stern drive.

Grease the Fittings

Locate and wipe all grease fittings clean so the introduction of new grease doesn't force dirt and other grit into the bearing instead of vice versa. Old, dried-up grease causes wear while new grease lubricates and expels moisture. Pump the gun until you see new grease squirt out.

Restated for emphasis, the new lube expels trapped moisture preventing it from freezing, expanding and cracking the housing during sub-zero temperatures. If any of the fittings refuse to accept grease, remove them and soak them in solvent. If they still don't break free and accept grease, replace them. Once finished, wipe excess grease from the fittings so they don't attract dirt.

Important note: Whenever lubricating the transom end of the steering cable, first retract it into its housing. Otherwise, the grease job could cause hydraulic lock.

Inboard Marine Engines Only

After the engine has cooled down from the test run, plug the exhaust pipes to prevent moist air from migrating into the cylinders. Some old timers stuff oily rags in the holes, but a sock stuffed in a baggy works just as well. Pack the rags in tight enough in the exhaust outlet so they stay in place. Which means insert them deeply enough into the cavity to secure them in place, but not so far they're difficult to extract.

Disconnect the propeller shaft coupling where it joins the transmission to avoid undue stress on the connection. Come spring, launch uncoupled, check alignment and re-couple. This procedure harkens back to the days of wooden hulls which tended to flex more in their cradles than today's fiberglass hulls. Assuming good cradling, it's probably not necessary to go to all that trouble. If in doubt, don't hesitate to consult the builder.

Either way, wipe the shaft and its coupling surfaces with an oily rag to protect against corrosion. Then re-pack the stuffing box at the shaft and rudders. Lay a wrench on each of the stuffing box bolts making sure they haven't vibrated loose. Tighten as necessary.

Check the exhaust system for metal that's rusted through. Also be alert for any loose clamps and bolts. Inspect the hull's underwater zincs, replacing any that have corroded away to less than 2/3 of their original size. Also be sure to check the zinc anodes in the cooling system; there may be as many as three or four. If you're not sure of their number and location, refer to the owner's manual.

Battery Care

Detailed Battery care during lay-up extends its life. The reality that it's an unglamorous job is tempered somewhat by the fact that there isn't much to the process. Once you've cleaned up the beast a bit and greased its posts, all you need do is keep the cell plates covered with water and charged. For safety's sake, always wear gloves and goggles when a working with batteries.

Begin by checking the state of charge with a hydrometer. As a battery charges it pulls acid out of the battery plates and puts it back into the electrolyte solution. When specific gravity drops below 1.230 (too much water, not enough acid), charge the battery until the reading climbs to 1.260. When a battery refuses to come up to a full charge, it's on its last legs.

As a rule of thumb, its best to check water level and recharge about every 60 days. Trickle charge at about six amps for about five to six hours. Do not fast charge the battery. Since you're in the dead of winter, you're in no hurry to nuke it anyway. Besides, fast charging can cause low-maintenance batteries to loose water. In the extreme it can buckle battery plates, ruining the battery.

Keep in mind that as a battery loses its charge, its electrolyte becomes vulnerable to freezing. When it does freeze, the fluid will expand and crack the battery's case. Incidentally it's not true that placing a battery on a concrete floor makes it discharge quicker. This myth comes out of the old days when battery construction in general was so poor that they had a hard time holding a charge no matter where they were placed. Today's batteries are much better at holding a charge, but the myth lives on in spite of reality.

Once the engine has been fogged, remove the battery from the boat and wash the top of the case with a solution of either ammonia and water or baking soda and water. Be careful not to spill any of the solution into the cells or it will neutralize the electrolyte and weaken the battery permanently if not outright kill it. This one simple cleaning procedure prevents dirt on top of the battery from leaking voltage between the two terminals and draining the battery over the long winter months.

Wire brush or sandpaper the battery posts until they shine, then coat with grease. Top off each individual cell with distilled water and never tap water. Otherwise the mineral impurities shorten battery life. Charge the battery, then store it in a cool, dry place. Keep it away from excess heat, which means storage next to a furnace or water heater is not appropriate.

About every 45 days all winter long, check the water level and trickle charge. Automotive type trickle chargers must be check frequently and turned off when the battery reaches its full charge. Conversely, marine type battery charges are specifically designed to turn off when the battery is full of juice, and then turn back on as it discharges.

Cosmic Cosmetic Protection

Hose down the power plant and drive leg to wash away any dirt and salt spray that may have accumulated. If the engine is really grimy, first coat the affected surfaces with engine cleaning solvent. Give it time to work then follow-up with water.

If sand has scoured paint off the skeg, wash the surface in soap and water, scrub with a bristle brush, then rinse. Prime, then paint exposed metal on the drive leg to protect it from corrosion. Shake the aerosol paint can briskly for a full five minutes before spraying. Five minutes may seem like a long time, but anything less and the paint just doesn't mix well enough to do a good job.

When spraying, don't swish the can back and forth. Instead make one neat pass from right to left. This is the tack coat. Its job is to help the second coat stick better. Lay on the paint in several applications, pausing briefly between coats. If a run or sag forms on the finish, take a shop towel and daub it off. Let the paint dry, then sand down the rough edges and try again. Job completed, turn the can upside down and spray until no more paint comes out. This cleans the nozzle so it's not clogged up the next time you paint.

A word of caution: When touching up surfaces with a paint can, it's good practice to mask off the sacrificial zincs so over spray doesn't insulate these components from electrolytic activity and thereby render them useless as corrosion fighters.

Inspect the sacrificial zincs located on the outdrive. Little by little over the past season they've been eaten away by galvanic action. Tap each one with a hammer to dislodge consumed material. Replace them if they've been reduced to less than half their original size

Regardless of whether or not the zinc needs replacing, remove it and make sure there is good metal-to-metal contact between the zinc and the housing it's protecting. Otherwise it's worthless.

Before replacing, coat the bolt's threads with anti-corrosion lubricant so it doesn't corrode in place making later removal nearly impossible. If you're considering overlooking this simple procedure keep in mind unchecked galvanic action can eat away aluminum gear housing and cast iron engine blocks.

Safe Skegs

What about broken skeg tips and bent anti-ventilation plates: Can they be repaired? Because aluminum is very hard to work with any repairs are best left to the experts. You should know heli-arc welding is very expensive and the process often warps the gear case, kinking shaft and bearing loads causing premature wear if not outright failure. Sorry.

Oil and Filter:
Change Them

Drain crankcase oil hot so all the acids and other impurities are stirred up and floating in suspension. When the dirty, old oil drains out into the pain, so too does the acids and impurities. On the other hand, if you procrastinate and don't change engine oil at lay-up, those same acids spend the winter etching the engine's machined surfaces, accelerating wear and decreasing longevity. For the same reason it's important to change the oil filter at the same time crankcase lube is changed. Otherwise a quart of dirty oil (from the old filter) contaminates the new. Be sure to dispose of the old crankcase oil in an environmentally responsible manner.

Pre-fill the new oil filter so on start-up the crankshaft bearings get an immediate supply of lubricant instead of having to wait for the pump to first fill the filter and then route oil to the galleys. After all, if the filter is dry, so are the bearings. Smear a fingerful of oil around the filter gasket so it seals better against the block.

Consider having the engine oil analyzed. a lab report can be invaluable, detailing the presence or absence, of metal particles in the crankcase. And it can affirm that all the bearing, crankshaft journals and pistons are in good heath for in the coming season.

Water Pumps

What about water pumps, should you open up a watch that's still ticking away as smoothly as a Swiss watch? Maybe, may be not. As impellers age, their rubber hardens. That reduction in flexibility impairs the pump's ability to circulate water throughout the cooling system. One by one the little legs crack at the hub, then break off. Eventually coolant flow stops altogether. The bad news is that all this happens inside the engine where you can't see it.

So how about a pre-emptive strike? Disassembling a water pump during lay-up allows you to determine the condition of the impeller in a safe haven instead of offshore. Water pumps located in outboard motor and stern drive lower units require minor dis assembly. So consider working smarter, not harder by replacing the impeller outright every two or three years.

Furthermore, because realigning a lower unit's drive-shaft and cooling tubes can be very difficult, this is a job best left to a certified marine mechanic. Inboard marine engines with an easily accessible water pump should have theirs taken apart and inspected. Impellers with stiff impeller vanes should be discarded and replaced. Also be sure to check the impeller housing surfaces for scoring that reduces raw water flow. It also follows that lay-up is an opportune time to make sure the spare parts kits contains and extra impeller are on board.

Freshwater and
Closed Cooling

Backwash the cooling system to rid it of salt, sediment and rust flakes. Newer model stern drives and outboards come with a garden hose attachment built-in. Older models require the ubiquitous earmuff style flushette that clamps onto the water intake.

Depending on your locale, it may be a good idea to pump a gallon of anti-freeze into the cooling system to prevent minuscule ice pockets from forming and cracking the block. To prevent contaminating the environment be sure to use EPA approved antifreeze.

When finished, facilitate complete draining of the low spots in the engine by tipping the bow higher than the stern. In the end when you remove the drain plugs from the engine block and manifolds, store them in a plastic baggy along with the ignition keys so they'll be easy to find in the spring. Some stern drives and outboards can be flushed with the engine off. However, a majority require the engine to be running so the water pump can circulate fresh water to all the nooks and crannies in the cooling system. When in doubt, read the owner's manual or consult the manufacturer. Heat exchangers should be removed and cleaned about every other year. Otherwise corrosion flakes and salt crystals could impair the transfer of heat out of the engine.

Also, in order to preclude accidental contact with a turning propeller, it's best to remove it before flushing the engine. Remove the drain plugs from the block and store them in a plastic bag along with the ignition keys.

Test coolant with a hydrometer, making sure the blend exhibits adequate antifreeze protection. Top off as necessary. If the coolant has aged more than two years, the anti-freeze/water solution may have lost its corrosion-fighting ability. Antifreeze's primary function is to prevent engine coolant from freezing, expanding and cracking heads and the block wide open. Just as important, an antifreeze blend includes ingredients that also prevent internal corrosion. And the reason we change it every year or so is because over time antifreeze gradually looses this anti-corrosion fighting ability by becoming acidic. Great. So how do we know when to change coolant without guessing? It's easier than you think.

One expedient method for checking coolant's acidity is with a voltmeter. Set the meter on its 1/10th volt scale and dip one probe into the coolant and attach the other to the coolant reservoir's ground. Acidic, or corrosive, coolant acts exactly like battery electrolyte and produces an electrical charge. As a rule of thumb, if the voltmeter reads less than .80 volts, the coolant is still non-corrosive. However, if the meter reads higher than .80 volts, then the coolant has turned acidic and should be flushed and replaced. Whenever in doubt, drain and refill with a 50/50 blend of antifreeze and water. Be sure to dispose of the old antifreeze in an environmentally responsible manner. Do not make the mistake of topping off with Reverse Osmosis water, it is mineral starved and can corrode an engine from the inside out.

Steering and Throttle Shift Controls

Check the steering by cranking the wheel hard to part, then hard to starboard. The wheel should traverse freely in both directions. With the rig out of the water and the engine off, run the throttle up and down to make sure there is no binding. Shifting into forward and reverse should lock up the propeller tight. It should not ratchet or spin freely. Conversely, in neutral it should free-wheel, but not lockup or ratchet. If there is any deviation from this pattern, consult your service technician.

Inspect the shift and throttle cables. If either one binds or shows cracked outer casing, it should be replaced.

The Outboard Motor Powerhead

Thoroughly inspect the outboard motor's power head Check the rubber fuel line for cracks or breaks. Pay extra close attention to hose nearest the engine, where heat accelerates deterioration. This component should be supple and flexible. If a line feels mushy or bloated, or exhibit cracks, replace it.

Similarly, check the primer bulb making sure it's rubber hasn't stiffened with age. It should work freely. If the hose connectors are leaky, replace them now. Dangling cowling rubbers can be glued back in place with weather-strip compound. Snug tight any loose bolts you may find, being careful not to strip the sensitive aluminum threads. On smaller outboards be sure to lubricate the hold down clamps that secure the motor to the transom.

Begin by stabilizing the gasoline, halting its transformation into gum and varnish. Otherwise, by springtime the carburetor may be so plugged up the engine won't start. This procedure is even more important nowadays because gasoline shelf life has become so short: After ninety days untreated fuel turns sour. The exact quantity of stabilizer required depends upon two variables: How many gallons need to be treated and for many months. The larger the volume of fuel and the longer the spell of time, the more ounces of stabilizer required. Follow the instructions printed on the can, and wear rubber gloves.

Backwash the cooling system with a garden hose adapter, flushing out salt, sediment, and rust flakes that would otherwise corrode the cooling system. Where appropriate, remove sea water impellers. If you're unsure whether your model of inboard or stern drive would benefit from this step, consult your owners manual. Important to note, heat exchanger tubes should be removed and cleaned every other year. Also check to see whether your engine should be running or turned-off while back washing. Rust-proof cylinder walls by fogging their surfaces with a super-sticky oil. With the engine idling, shut off its fuel supply so its running on just the fuel in the carburetor's float bowl. Just as it starts to die, squirt fogging oil down the carburetor throat. Flood the engine with fogging oil until it stops running. Next remove all of the spark plugs and dump about an ounce of fogging oil into each cylinder. With the spark plugs back in place (finger tight) and the ignition disabled, crank the engine for fifteen seconds.

Loosen water pump, alternator and power steering drive belt, to lessen the tension on those component's bearings. Inspect the drive belts for cracks or frayed edges. Replace as necessary. Grease the steering linkage, shift cable, tilt mechanisms, and swivel points. Zerk fittings that won't take lube should be unscrewed and replaced. Greasing expels water preventing it freezing, expanding and breaking parts. On inboards and stern drive motors, remove the carburetor flame arrestor and soak it in kerosene. Air dry then reinstall. Drain the gear case oil. Otherwise, trapped water could freeze, expand and break the housing. First remove the bottom drain plug, then the top. A gallon plastic milk jug with its top hacked-off makes a good expedient drain pan. Examine the dirty oil for water, bits of broken gear teeth and bronze shavings. If any are present, consult a marine mechanic for repairs. Assuming all is well, refill the lower unit with the factory recommended lubricant. Fill from the bottom. When lubricant spills out the top hole, the housing is full. Insert the top drain plug first. Make certain each drain plug has one and only one gasket, and that no gasket is lodged in the casting's recess.

During the course of the winter, unprotected cylinder walls rust. In minor cases the oxidation attacks piston rings and cylinder walls foreshortening engine life. In severe cases the parts rusts solid, locking up the engine so that it won't even turn over. When that happens dis-assembly is the only available cure. Prevention of this malady involves a simple technique known as fogging, or coating the cylinder walls with a sticky, preservative oil that won't easily slide off a cylinder wall or piston ring.

Outboard motors should be stored in the down position in order to prevent strain on the lift unit seals

Spring Commissioning

The first step in spring commissioning is simple as the sea is salt: Review the lay-up procedures followed last fall. Now simply undo whatever procedures were undertaken last autumn.

This is an opportune time to bring the battery up to a full charge one last time before launching. Be sure to check the fluid level in each of the individual cells, making sure it hasn't dropped down below the top of the plates. Otherwise the plates will sulphate when they come into contact with the air, seriously shortening the battery's lifespan. Make sure battery bank posts and terminals are squeaky clean and snugged down tight.

Even though last fall you painstakingly drained and filled the gear case and changed the engine crankcase oil, to be on the safe side, recheck the fluid levels guaranteeing you don't accidentally run an engine or drive without lubricant in the sump. Similarly run the outdrive up and down through several cycles, then recheck the lift pump's fluid level.

Inspect propeller blades for nicks and dings, straightening dings with a rawhide mallet and filing minor nicks smooth, removing as little metal as possible to prevent unbalancing the wheel. Examine the propeller's shock absorber bushing for cracks or other damage.

Inspect sacrificial zincs and replace any corroded away to less than half their original size. Remove every individual zinc and make sure there's good metal-to-metal contact between it and its mating surface.

Remove any oily rags stuffed in place to block wet air from flowing into the engine intake or exhaust.

On gas engines remove the spark plugs that were intentionally left in place, finger tight. Wipe them dry of fogging oil. With the coil wire unplugged and the throttle wide open, crank the engine through several revolutions, blowing the fogging oil out of the cylinders. Cranking the engine through several revolutions not only pre lubes the crankshaft and camshaft bearings, it also fills the carburetor float bowl. The procedure virtually assures the engine will start quickly and with sufficient lubrication. Make sure the spark plug terminals are dry, then replace them and their ignition wire boots.

Tip: If you didn't tune the engine last fall, this is a good time to replace the spark plugs. At a minimum, gap the old spark plugs before replacing. Check the engine for loose, missing, or damaged parts, laying a wrench on each and every nut and bolt including engine mounts and manifold bolts. Make sure none have vibrated loose, including the steering linkage.

Before snugging alternator and water-pump drive belts again, inspect for cracks, checkering, or frays. Correct tension allows for about one-fourth to three-eighths inch play measured midway between the pulleys.

After checking for checks or cracks, grab each cooling-system hose; any that are hard, brittle, or bulged, replace. Check hose clamps for corrosion, damage, or looseness.

Grease all the zerk fittings to expel moisture that may have accumulated. Dose fuel with additives for absorbing water and freshening fuel. Replace engine block drain plugs.

Test run the engine. If it doesn't start right up after a couple turns of the crank, don't mindlessly run the battery down: Instead, troubleshoot. Once running, let the engine idle until it reaches its normal temperature to evaporate any moisture.

Monitor oil pressure and temperature as the engine continues to warm up. Check the oil filter base for leaks and looseness. Eyeball the engine block and manifolds. Often cooling system leaks can be spotted by the telltale rust stain streaking down the side of the block. Follow the rust upstream to pinpoint its source. Another cooling system tip, when you run first run up the engine in the spring, keep an eye out for steam vapor which could be another clue something has gone amiss with the cooling system. Look for coolant leaks, especially in the drain plugs you just reinstalled--steam vapor means you're loosing coolant.

Finished for the day? Make a written record of everything.

Remove the spark plugs, then crank the engine for about a minute to blow the fogging oil out of the cylinders. If the plugs weren't changed last fall, do so now, then re-install. On stern drives and inboards with closed cooling systems, check coolant. Also, if the anti-freeze blend is more than two seasons old, drain and refill so the accumulated acid content won't corrode the internal passages in the engine.

Examine drive belts for proper tension and damage. Squeeze every cooling and fuel line hose. They should be supple, but not mushy or rock hard. If any are, replace. Also check the hose clamps, making sure corrosion hasn't weakened the. If not already double-clamped, spring commissioning is an opportune time to do so.

On stern drives and inboards, yank the dipstick and check crankcase oil level. Also check trim\tilt and power steering pump reservoirs, topping off as necessary. Lay a wrench on every nut and bolt you can find, making sure none of the power head's fasteners vibrated loose last season.

Double check the gear oil. Make sure it's full of lubricant and not water.

Grease every Zerk fitting in sight, expelling water and dirt and protecting against friction wear.

Remove the propeller and coat the prop shaft with marine grade, corrosion resistant grease.

Inspect the propeller for damage. Make sure a spare propeller is stowed in the parts locker. If sand has scoured paint and left bare metal showing, clean the surface, the prime and follow up with at least one finish coat.

Examine the sacrificial zincs, replacing any that have corroded away to less than half their original size. Do not grease zinc retaining bolts, otherwise good electrical connection will be lost and the corrosion fighting ability with it.

Run the trim/tilt up an down through several cycles to make sure it's working properly. Lay a wrench on the lift ram's hydraulic lines making sure they are tight.

Crank the steering wheel from port to starboard and back again to make sure it to is functioning.

Begin spring commissioning by reviewing exactly which lay-up procedures were performed last fall. Bring the starting and deep cycle batteries up to full charge. Remove the spark plugs, then crank the engine for about a minute to blow the fogging oil out of the cylinders. If the plugs weren't changed last fall, do so now, then re-install.

On stern drives and inboards with closed cooling systems, check coolant. Also, if the anti-freeze blend is more than two seasons old, drain and refill so the accumulated acid content won't corrode the internal passages in the engine.

Examine drive belts for proper tension and damage.

Squeeze every cooling and fuel line hose. They should be supple, not mushy or rock hard. If any are, replace. Also check the hose clamps, making sure corrosion hasn't weakened any. If not already double-clamped, spring commissioning is an opportune time to do so.

Also check trim/tilt and power steering pump reservoirs, topping off as necessary. Lay a wrench on every nut and bolt you can find, making sure none of the power head's fasteners vibrated loose last season.

Consult your owner's manual to locate all the grease fittings. Wipe them clean before greasing to avoid pumping dirt into the mechanism. Grease every Zerk fitting in sight, expelling water and dirt and protecting against friction wear. Pump in grease until the dirty grease and water are expelled. Hint: Look for the appearance of clean grease.

Remove the propeller and coat the propeller shaft with marine grade, corrosion resistant grease. Inspect the propeller for damage.

Make sure a spare propeller is stowed in the parts locker. If sand has scoured paint and left bare metal showing, clean the surface, the prime and follow up with at least one finish coat.

Examine the sacrificial zincs, replacing any that have corroded away to less than half their original size. Do not grease zinc retaining bolts, otherwise good electrical connection will be lost and the corrosion fighting ability with it.

Run the trim/tilt up an down through several cycles to make sure it's working properly. Lay a wrench on the lift ram's hydraulic lines making sure they are tight.

Crank the steering wheel from port to starboard and back again to make sure it to is functioning. Further Resources

Mid-Summer checklist

Mid-season checklists are traditional and traditionally ignored. The reason is founded in human nature. Precious leisure time, spent huddled under the engine cover, might better be enjoyed on the water. On the other hand, should a neglected marine engine fail, you're cruising nowhere this weekend. For this reason one really ought to give the engine and drive the once-over somewhere in the middle of the boating season. This can avoid trouble that might be waiting in the wings. Therefore, we offer a minimalist dream, a bare bones, mid-season checklist appropriate for both diesel and gas engines.

Begin by checking vital fluid levels. Pull the dipstick on stern drives and inboards. If the crankcase oil is low, consider having a marine mechanic find out why. On closed cooling systems, top off the coolant.

Check starting and deep-cycle battery electrolyte levels. Top off with distilled water only, became tap water often contains minerals which shorten battery life. If any cell requires more than an ounce of water, find out why. Inspect battery terminals for tightness and for corrosion. Loose, green-encrusted battery cables might rob enough voltage to cause hard starting, or no starting.

Check fluid levels on the transmission or outdrive as well as on a diesel engine's supercharger oil (when so equipped). On outdrives, look for signs of water in the gear oil that means a propeller shaft or drive shaft seal has failed. It only takes a minute to crack the lower drain screw and let a drop or two leak out.

Barely crack the bottom drain screw and see what fluid trickles out. Since oil floats, if there is water present, that's what you'll see at the first turn of the screw. An obvious exception: If the engine has been recently run, the oil and water will have emulsified, looking like a chocolate brown froth.

On stern drives and outboard motors, raise up the drive leg and look at the propeller. Its leading edges should be clean, and unbroken by dings and gouges. Similarly, none of the blades should be bent. A zealot would remove the propeller and make sure no monofilament is wrapped around the propeller shaft. Fish line is notorious for worming its way in through the gear case seal, destroying it in the process.

Check the fluid level on the trim/tilt pump, topping off as necessary. If it needs more than an ounce, schedule repairs. On outboards, it's not a bad idea to make sure the transom mounting bolts are tight. Vibration might have worked them loose.

Assuming you've logged sufficient hours (consult the owner's manual for details), replace crankcase oil, plus fuel and water-separation filters. Where appropriate (some diesels), also change the air filter and PCV valve.

While not critical, and assuming thorough spring commissioning, it's still a good idea to eyeball sacrificial zincs. The reason isn't the age of the zincs. Instead, its due to the fact that dockside voltage leaks can eat away zincs and leave you unprotected in a very short time. So, inspect zincs both inside the engine coolant systems and on propeller shafts and other submerged components. Once zincs have shrunken away to less than half their original dimensions, remove and replace.

Warning: never use anti-seize lubricant, paints, sealers, or pipe dope when installing zincs. To do so isolates them electrically from the metal they're meant to protect. Corrosion would quickly follow. If you're not sure where all the sacrificial zincs are located, consult your owners manual.

Since you're climbing around the engine room, inspect engine mating surfaces where flanges are bolted to the block (water pumps, raw water piping, etc.). If there's liquid escaping (oil or water), replace the gaskets before the problem gets worse (Read: more expensive to fix). If there are hot spots visible (discolored paint) check for blockages or corrosion in the component itself. Check alternator and water-pump belt tension and overall condition. Replace any belt that's frayed or cracked. Similarly, squeeze water hoses. They should be supple, never rigid, crumbling or cracked.

Make sure fuel in the bowl of the water separator is clear, not cloudy. Consider dosing the fuel with an appropriate drier to remove water that's built up from condensation forming on the sides of the fuel tanks.

On gensets take special care to be sure siphon breaks are clean and that water-lift muffler connections are secure. Make sure the bilge pump is operational.

Finally, crack open the onboard tool kit and spare parts cache to make sure it's fully stocked. At a minimum, you should be able to change a propeller, spark plugs and drive belts. You should also have onboard oil and fuel filters plus enough lubricant to change crankcase oil. Grease, duct tape and WD-40 will also come in handy. On the environmental side, lay away a stock of oil-absorbing socks or powders on board to deal with any fuel that you might spill.

Tune-up In A Can

Thanks to advance in ignition systems most will keep an engine running great or it won't run at all. So when an engine runs poorly chances are good what's gone wrong is either the spark plugs or the combustion chamber. In both cases carbon fouling is the culprit causing hard starting and poor fuel economy. The good news is these power-robbing, engine-wearing deposits are expeditiously removed by means of internal engine cleaner. In fact the inexpensive cure is so simple to apply that it's almost laughable. Some folks around the marine circuit call it Tune-Up-In-A-Can.

To use it start the engine and run it until the dash gauge indicates normal operating temperature. On inboards and stern drives remove the flame arrestor giving you a straight shot down the carburetor. Squirt internal engine cleaner down the carburetor intake. Wash the throttle plates and on inboard and stern drives, the venturi cluster. Use the straw-like nozzle to shoot the aerosol deep into the carburetor's throat. Load the engine down with great gobs of the stuff until great clouds of white, stinky, smoke billow forth from the exhaust. Keep squirting. The engine will sputter and threaten to die. Keep it running a moment longer, than bog the engine down with about two ounces of the cleaner until it dies.

When it does, let the chemicals work for about an hour in a process that's akin to oven cleaner. The chemicals will do their dirty work, loosening up the carbon and other fouling deposits from the piston domes and combustion chambers.

After an hour or so, crank the engine. Expect hard starting

followed by rough running before the power plant smooths out. Expect sputtering for a minute or two as it coughs out all the junk that's been choking fuel efficiency. Soon the old power plant should be purring like a well-oiled wheel.

If the engine refuses to start, don't drain the battery in a valiant attempt to get it going. Instead, work smarter, not harder. Remove all of the spark plugs and one by one dry the insulators with a blast of compressed air or a shop towel. Before replacing, crank the engine through a couple of revolutions to blow the excess internal engine cleaner out of the cylinders. Now the beast will roar to life.

This better living through chemistry method of blowing the cobs out of an internal combustion engine dates back to the murky shadows of history. Old timers like to reminisce about how they used to pour a cup of water into the air horn of a Ford Model-T automobile to accomplish the same thing. And the Army Air Corp manuals dating back to the Second World War specify the same treatment for the big reciprocating radial engines of the B-29 super fortress bombers. Nevertheless, while spraying internal engine cleaner into an engine may seem like an unsophisticated method for problem solving, one thing's for sure. The method works.

Another method is to simply dose the fuel with Chevron's Techron fuel additive. It's readily available in automotive parts stores and all the Marts. Read the label to find out how many ounces are appropriate. You can also just buy 89 octane Chevron gas, which of course includes Techron as one of its additives. The Techron cure takes about a full tank of gas to get the job done.

The Ten Minute Tune-up

Tune-ups used to be complicated. For example, on an outboard mechanics had to first remove the flywheel in order to change or adjust ignition points. then once tuned, special test wheels had to be installed on the propeller shaft so the motor could be run under load in a test tank in order that a carburetor's high-speed circuit could be accurately adjusted. Such procedures took time, which inflated labor charges. Fortunately, advances in technology have made tune-ups much simpler and, hopefully, less expensive.

Most modern marine engines come with electronic ignition, which means there are no breaker points to fiddle with. Which in turn means the modern tune-up consists of little more than changing the spark plugs.

Start the ten minute tune-up by removing the spark plugs one at a time. As you remove them, examine each plug's insulator and electrode. The color and condition of the deposits reveal overall engine health. So what should the spark plug look like? The insulator should be colored a light chocolate brown, which means the fuel to air mix is correct.

If the insulator is white, the engine is running lean and that can be due to incorrect ignition timing or carburetor adjustment.

Carbon fouling is a dull-black, dry, sooty deposit. Primary include prolonged idling, a weak ignition spark, an out of adjustment carburetor, a stuck float valve, a sticky choke, a clogged or dirty spark arrestor, out of whack ignition point gap, incorrect ignition timing.

Wet black, oily deposits in combination with bluish exhaust smoke and oil consumption points to a serious mechanical problem. Stuck rings, worn rings or worn valves guides are likely culprits.

Gapping the plugs close to their specifications, .035" for example, keeps an engine in tune longer.

Low-maintenance motors, like MerCruiser Scorpion inboards and stern drives, merely require changing vital fluids and filters. The spark plugs are nearly indestructible. On most other inboards, stern drives and outboards, tune-ups only require changing the spark plugs.

How to Rebuild an Outboard Carburetor

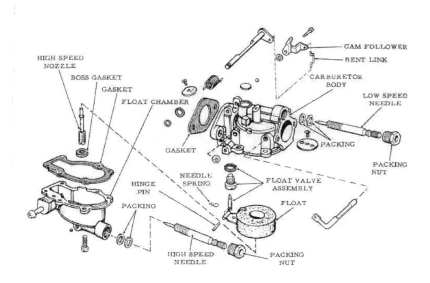

THERE'S A WAY TO REBUILD AN OUTBOARD CARBURETOR that not many boat owners are aware of. Most people simply go out and buy a new one. It's no secret that gasoline has a short shelf life. After even a few weeks the lighter molecules evaporate, leaving behind sticky fuel that gums up float bowls and clogs narrow jets and passages. But in a couple of hours you can make your carburetor function like new. One tip is to shoot photos along the way as a memory aid during reassembly.

Detach the primer bulb fuel line from the engine. Under the cowling, disconnect the fuel line that runs to the carburetor.

Disconnect linkage connecting the carburetor to the engine. Unbolt the carburetor from the intake manifold--there are usually two bolts. Disassemble the carburetor and lay out the parts on a clean shop towel.

Inspect the float valve needle. Its up and down motion lets fuel in or shuts off the flow. If the needle's tip is grooved, gas trickles in no matter what the position of the float. This overflow richens the fuel-to-air mix, causing rough running and wasting fuel. Needle and seat come as a set. When buying it bring the make, model number and serial number of the engine to the parts counter. Also buy an aerosol can of carburetor cleaner (make sure it has a red straw taped to its side). You may want to buy an entire rebuild kit, but check what parts are included and how they match yours.

Shake the float. It's hollow and it should be empty. If there's fuel inside, it leaks and extra liquid weight drags the needle down, constantly flowing fuel. Sometimes a new float is included in a rebuild kit. The gasket between the float bowl and the carburetor body can be reused, but it's wise to replace it. Similarly, always replace the paper gasket or O-ring between the carburetor base and the intake manifold. If it leaks air the engine runs lean.

Remove all of the jets from the carburetor body. Work carefully. If your screwdriver's blade doesn't exactly fit the brass jet's slot then drive to the store and buy one that does. Otherwise, you may damage the jet even if you get it out. Next, don rubber gloves and eye protection. Work in an area with lots of fresh air, but minimal breeze. Insert the little red straw in the carb cleaner's spray nozzle.

Spray the float bowl and the underside of the carb body. Then insert the straw into every passage and orifice you see and spray it. Don't forget the expansion plug passages (see "Top Secret"). The cleaner is a solvent that rapidly dissolves gum and varnish. The pressurized flow blows dissolved gook out of the castings. When everything has been sprayed, reassemble the parts. Refer to those photos you took.

Many correctly executed outboard carb jobs work well for an hour or two, then go sour and the engine reverts to rough running. The reason is that when carburetors are manufactured, tiny passages are drilled in the aluminum casting. But they're overlooked when cleaning. Locate the expansion plug on your carburetor (see diagram). The passages are hidden behind the plug. Secure the carb body on the bench. Carefully use a hammer to drive the tip of a narrow blade screwdriver into the plug and lever it out.

Accessing those passages allows them to be unclogged by spraying carb cleaner into them. You'll need a new plug along with liquid sealer, both available from the engine's manufacturer. Slather the sides of the plug with sealant and slip it into place. Carefully drive it into its bore with a mallet and then a small socket until you feel it bottom out in the casting.

Ten Top Causes
Of Marine Engine Breakdown

It doesn't happen often, but when an engine does break down at sea, your day on the water takes a serious turn for the worse. If you're familiar with the most common causes of engine failure, however, you can cut down the chances you'll be a victim of a breakdown. Here are 10 to watch out for.

1. NO FUEL: Incredible as it may sound, a boat's fuel tank can be as dry as a bone--even when the gauge claims there's plenty in reserve. This makes sense when you realize that at different speeds and loads a hull operates at different angles so there is no true level for the sending unit to reference. You can avoid running out of fuel by installing one of the new fuel-management systems offered by marine-engine manufacturers--systems like Mercury's SmartCraft, Yamaha's Command Link and others--that communicate with the engine, monitoring fuel flow at the point of consumption. Besides displaying gallons available until empty, engine-management systems reveal optimal cruising rpm for best mileage. They also signal possible trouble if fuel consumption suddenly soars. Another option is an aftermarket flow meter available from FloScan (www.floscan.com).

2. DIRTY FUEL: Engine problems are also caused by dirt and water in the fuel. Debris, stirred up from the bottom of the tank by wave action, is drawn into the fuel line and clogs the fuel filter element. Starved for fuel, the engine begins to run poorly, and then not at all. A simple solution is to retrofit a vacuum gauge to the fuel/water separator so you'll know when it's time

to swap filter elements. Water in the fuel can drive you mad. Moisture condenses out of the highly humid air on the inside walls of a fuel tank, then runs down into the fuel. Water can also be introduced at the fuel dock from a contaminated fuel supply. Either way, the fuel floats on top of the water, so it's the water that's pulled into the engine, causing it to stumble and die. A fuel/water separator protects against this by handily extracting the water. Just remember to check the bowl daily and drain off the accumulated water. For severe contamination, dose the fuel supply with a fuel-drying additive.

3. FUEL BUGS: Diesel engines suffer from "bugs" literally growing in the fuel. If left unchecked, these critters clog filters. Prevention is nothing more complicated than using additives that kill the bugs and convert them into a combustible product. Additives that only kill the bugs are insufficient because the corpses fall to the bottom of the tank as sediment, waiting for the day they can plug up the filters. Also, by means of an induced electrical charge, fuel-conditioning devices like Algae-X (www.algae-x.net) break up clusters of hydrocarbons into particles that burn completely in the combustion process. Adding such a device will alleviate microbial contamination problems.

4.TIRED PUMP: A worn-out circulating water pump is another engine killer. Impellers are commonly made of nitrile, a rubber-like compound that stiffens over time. Hardened blades take a set, or break off entirely, and hardened or missing blades reduce coolant flow. On inboards and some stern drives, the water pump is easily accessible and features an inspection cover that can be removed. Lost blades are easy to detect. Hardened blades can be felt. Engine manufacturers all have impeller kits to remedy the problem.

5. HARD HOSE: As hoses age they lose their resiliency and collapse, causing a restriction in the flow of engine coolant. This results in over-heating, the most common source of engine failure. When the water pump sucks water from a through-hull via a collapsed hose, the engine, starved for coolant, overheats. Prevention is simple: Visually inspect cooling hoses and squeeze them to be sure they retain their shape and set.

6. CLOGGED INTAKE: Another culprit that causes overheating is floating debris in the water. Flotsam and jetsam--things like discarded plastic baggies--can plug up the raw-water intake. You can avoid this problem on boats equipped with a raw-water strainer by periodically inspecting the strainer basket. When removing debris, be sure to properly replace the seal, otherwise the pump will lose suction. Some mechanics smear the seal with a generous dab of Vaseline petroleum jelly or marine-grade grease for extra sealing power.

7. HARD KNOCKS: If you collide with an underwater obstacle, the result can be destroyed or bent propeller blades. A blade can be severed entirely, or metal may be missing. If you make the mistake of trying to get back to port with a severely damaged prop, the vibration generated can compound the damage by breaking a propeller shaft. The solution is to carry a spare prop, although changing an inboard's prop on the water can be a major proposition. On outboards and stern drives, if the main wheel is a pricey stainless one, consider a cheaper aluminum backup. Some brands feature replaceable blades. As long as the hub is undamaged, a single blade or blades can be swapped right on the water.

8. BAD BATTERY: Marine starting batteries die from old age and neglect. The best advice here is to keep terminals and posts clean. That green corrosion that builds up restricts the flow of current, preventing the cells from fully charging. Flooded cell batteries need occasional topping off with distilled water to keep the electrolyte healthy. During lay-up, consider having your battery tested to determine its condition and expected longevity.

9. STALE FUEL: Gasoline has a short shelf life. In mere weeks it can become sticky, fouling fuel filters and plugging the fine passages of a carburetor. (Fuel-injected engines are immune because in the fuel lines gas remains under pressure and not exposed to oxygen.) To prevent problems, whenever the engine will remain idle for more than two weeks, add fuel stabilizer and run the engine before leaving it idle. The shorter the lay-up term, the lower the volume of the canned cure required. In season, that usually means a much smaller dose than during lay-up.

10. SAGGING BELT: Drive belts don't have to break to cause problems. As V-belts wear, they stretch and begin to slip. Consequently, alternators and water pumps don't spin to their full speed. Batteries may not fully charge and coolant circulates sluggishly. The solution is to check belt tension regularly and tighten belts when necessary. Drive belts also snap. The only way to avoid this malady is to replace them once they begin to show wear. Always carry spare belts so that if one should snap unexpectedly, you can replace it.

Marine Engine Enemies

Any marine mechanic worth his paycheck will readily admit that few engines die of old age. It's neglect that usually does them in. When an engine sits without being run, cylinder walls rust, pit and then score the piston rings. Poor maintenance causes hoses to collapse, the engine to overheat and the block to crack. Or, junk fuel clogs a fuel injector and the distorted spray pattern torches the piston dome.

These are old scenarios. A newer one involves watermakers, which can indirectly kill a marine engine. A watermaker, with its reverse-osmosis membranes, can scrub saltwater squeaky clean for drinking, but when added to an engine's expansion tank, reverse-osmosis-generated water attacks copper and gray iron castings. Components like temperature senders dissolve in the mineral-starved water. One case history documented by Seattle-based Northern Lights reveals how reverse-osmosis-generated water dissolved about a dozen senders in a row before the warranty team figured out the problem. There have been cases where cylinder liners eroded completely through in just 300 engine hours. But don't despair--there's a simple solution. According to Dick Gee of Northern Lights, "The only fluid that belongs in the coolant blend, besides antifreeze, is de-ionized distilled water."

Another engine issue is emissions. In the U.S., diesel fuel is supposed to be a minimum of 40 cetane (cetane is to diesel what octane is to gas). Engine manufacturers prefer 45-cetane fuel because lower-cetane diesel doesn't completely combust, creating exhaust smoke and smell. The white cloud stings the eyes, but it doesn't cause engine damage.

Unfortunately, diesel blends pumped at many fuel docks don't measure up. Testers from Northern Lights visited 20 marinas in Southern California. None of the diesel fuel met the 40-cetane minimum. One solution is to dose the diesel with a cetane booster available from companies like Northern Lights, MDR and Racor. Northern Lights (www.northern-lights.com) also has an inexpensive kit (shown above) with which you can test your fuel's cetane.

How to Survey Your Marine Engine

Lay-up is the perfect opportunity to survey your rig, to spot and repair faulty components before they fail and leave you between a rock and a reef. As rubber drive belts and hoses age, they deteriorate. Extreme temperatures, typical to marine installations, accelerate the wear beyond normal parameters. As we said earlier, lay-up is a prime opportunity to remove and replace borderline components.

Inspect drive belts for cracks, checkering or frayed edges. These flaws signal imminent failure. Replace as necessary. During lay-up belts should hang loose on their pulleys to reduce strain on water pump, alternator and power steering pump bearings and shafts. The strain could also stretch the belt, shortening its life.

Similarly, visually inspect the cooling system. knowing that overheating accounts for the majority of engine problems. This should come as no big surprise. Hoses are subjected to nearly 18 pounds per square inches of pressure. Engine room temperatures can near 280 degrees Fahrenheit. Corrosion mercilessly attacks heat exchangers and exhaust manifolds.

So what's the best way to check a hose? Look at it, then squeeze it. Begin with a visual inspection. Checkered or cracked surfaces indicate replacement is necessary. Squeeze each hose, hard. When a hose has lost its resilience or is bulged, replace it. It a hose feels lifeless, it's lost its strength and may swell or bust underway. On the other hand, if a hose has become hard and brittle, and lost its flexibility, engine vibration may shatter its fragile skin. Any that have lost resiliency and become hard and brittle or are have bulged require replacement

When leaks don't stop when a hose clamp is tightened, it's a good indication the hose has hardened and is about to fail. Don't pry off old hoses, Instead cut them off with a sharp knife to prevent damage to the inlet and outlet housings.

Look closely at each hose clamp to see whether any are corroded or otherwise damaged. Check a hose clamp by laying a screw driver on its screwhead, making sure it's tight and has not vibrated loose. If any are badly corroded, remove and replace. When one stubbornly refuses to come off, cut it off with tin snips. Use only stainless steel replacement hose clamps. Double clamp each connector to better guard against failure.

Inspect cooling system water hoses for cracking, bubbles or flaking. It's best to replace them now before it gets cold. Remove the raw-water impeller so that it doesn't take a set or freeze to the pump housing.

Notes to Self:

1. Anti-freeze protection registered as good down to ____ degrees Fahrenheit.

2. Engine block and exhaust manifold drain plugs are stored in: _____

3. **Lower Unit Tip:** Insure lower unit drain holes are unobstructed so water can freely drain. Otherwise trapped water could freeze solid and could crack the housing. Poke an appropriate piece of wire into the openings to make sure they are clear. Consult your owners manual to find the exact location of these holes.

4. Similarly, disconnect the speedometer pickup tube, allowing any trapped water to drip out. Then reconnect it when you're finished.

Stern Drive and Inboard Engine checklist:

☐   Grease steering and shift cable, Zerk fittings
☐   Inspect trim/tilt pump reservoir fluid level
☐   Inspect alternator and water pump drive belts
☐   Inspect cooling system hoses for damage
☐   Change the fuel filter
☐   Add gasoline stabilizer to the fuel tanks
☐   Run the engine to circulate stabilized fuel
☐   Shut down the engine
☐   Fog the cylinders with rust protectant
☐   Change crankcase oil and oil filter
☐   Charge then store the starting and deep cycle batteries
☐   Drain the block, manifold, circulation pump and coolers.
☐   Stern Drive and Outboard Motor Lower Units
☐   Check gimbal bearing (stern drives only)
☐   Change gear lube
☐   Grease all Zerk fittings
☐   Remove the propeller
☐   Grease the exposed propeller shaft
☐   Paint exposed metal on lower unit housing
☐   Outboard Motor Powerhead
☐   Check fuel line and primer bulb
☐   Replace the fuel filter
☐   Inspect alternator and power steering drive belt for damage
☐   Fog the cylinders

Outboard Motor Checklist

✓ Drain and fill gear case
✓ Grease power head and lower unit.
✓ Inspect steering connections.
✓ Inspect shift/throttle cables adjustment.
✓ Tune engine.
✓ Check rubber fuel line and primer bulb.
✓ Fog the engine.
✓ Check power trim/tilt fluid level.
✓ Charge and then store the starting and deep cycle batteries.

Stern Drive Checklist

- ☐   Drain and refill gear case
- ☐   Stabilize gasoline.
- ☐   Replace fuel filter.
- ☐   Change oil and filter.
- ☐   Grease U-joints and gimbal bearing.
- ☐   Tune engine.
- ☐   Inspect belts and hoses.
- ☐   Inspect steering linkage.
- ☐   Inspect shift/throttle cables adjustment.
- ☐   Test-run engine and fog.
- ☐   Drain cooling system.
- ☐   Charge and then store the starting and deep cycle batteries
- ☐   Fill engine with fresh anti-freeze.

Inboard Engine Checklist

- ☐   Stabilize gasoline.
- ☐   Replace fuel filter.
- ☐   Change engine oil and filter.
- ☐   Remove and clean spark arrestor
- ☐   Grease U-joints and gimbal bearing.
- ☐   Tune engine. Inspect belts and hoses.
- ☐   Inspect steering linkage.
- ☐   Inspect shift/throttle cables adjustment.
- ☐   Test-run engine
- ☐   Fog the cylinders Drain cooling system.
- ☐   Fill engine with anti-freeze.

Maintenance Record Form #1

Date action taken	
Complaint	
Corrective action taken	
Description of part replaced	
Replaced part cost	
Total parts cost.	
Total cost of repair	

Maintenance Record Form #2

Date action taken	
Complaint	
Corrective action taken	
Description of part replaced	
Replaced part cost	
Total parts cost.	
Total cost of repair	

Cylinder Compression Record

Cylinder Number	Reading	Date
1		
2		
3		
4		
5		
6		
7		
8		

Cylinder Number	Reading	Date
1		
2		
3		
4		
5		
6		
7		
8		

Oil Consumption Log

Engine #	Date of oil change	Engine Hours	Quarts Low	Quarts Added	Cost per quart	Cost per Filter	Total Cost (oil & filter)
							$
							$
							$

Fuel Stabilizing Log

Fuel tank #	Ounces of stabilizer	added to ____ gallons .	Date:

About the Author

The author, Timothy P. Banse, is a factory-trained marine mechanic and service manager who as a contributing editor wrote about marine engine technology and repairs for Motor Boating magazine for three decades as well as contributing stories to Popular Mechanics, and various Boating and Yachting magazines in the US, Australia, Singapore and Brazil. He has plied the trade in the Caribbean, Iowa, Arizona and California.

Made in the USA
San Bernardino, CA
01 October 2016